BOYS' TOYS

PLANES

SOURCEBOOKS, INC.
NAPERVILLE, ILLINOIS

Designer: WDA
Editor: Alison Moss
Researcher: Suzie Green

Sourcebooks, Inc.
P.O. Box 4410, Naperville, Illinois 60567-4410

(630) 961-3900
FAX: (630) 961-2168

Printed and bound in Hong Kong

MQ 10 9 8 7 6 5 4 3 2 1

ISBN: 1-57071-604-8

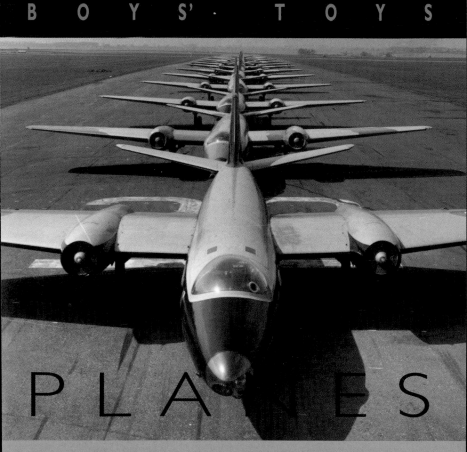

BOYS' · TOYS

PLANES

HULTON GETTY

INTRODUCTION

Icarus flew too close to the Sun and plummeted to his death. The great Leonardo da Vinci designed plans for a flying machine that undoubtedly would have worked had he lived to see it built, and hundreds of fools (mainly men) have leapt from bridges with homemade wings in the absolute belief that they could flap fast enough to defy nature. Since time began, men have wanted to fly. Then one day Orville Wright turned to his brother Wilbur and said he had a bright idea.

Once the Wright brothers proved that man could fly (if only for eleven seconds), they unleashed the biggest ego trip of them all—to be able to leave the ground and soar among the clouds. And the race to build the perfect airplane has been unrelenting—bigger; faster; stronger. Today's multimillion dollar jet fighters can travel to unimaginable speeds and heights—pushing man and machine to the very limits of physical and mental endurance.

Perhaps for us, that is what the allure of planes and flying is all about: to have one of those sleek, precision crafts responsive to our slightest touch; to have the skill and fortitude of the heroes of times past; to take command of the skies. Face it, what man does not secretly harbor the desire to be in the cockpit of a plane breaking the sound barrier or speeding his jet fighter through a 360 degree turn in midflight?

But there is also the romance. Today's airplanes are as beautiful a sight as the magnificent flying machines of the early days. Concorde racing down the runway or streaking across the sky is as awe inspiring as seeing the "Spirit of St. Louis"—the first plane to cross the Atlantic from Paris to New York. The first passenger airliners ferried eager travelers to distant lands in relative luxury; attractive flight attendants attended their every whim. Nowadays it is all so very different; jet liners are so fast that passengers can reach their destination almost before they have left their point of departure, and certainly before their luggage is found. And why is the experience of going into the cockpit of a holiday jet liner saved for a sulky six-year-old when you know that such an experience would be far more appreciated by someone of a more vintage generation.

Within the pages of this book you will find images of some of the great metal birds that have taken to the air, from air buses full of holiday-makers to the tools of military might. They evoke the romanticism of a bygone age, the roar of a jet engine, and the gentle hum of a propeller plane. They range from commercial airliners to air force bombers and jet fighters, including great names such as USAF-111, Northrup YF-17, Harrier, and Blackbird.

So sit back and enjoy. The sky is the limit.

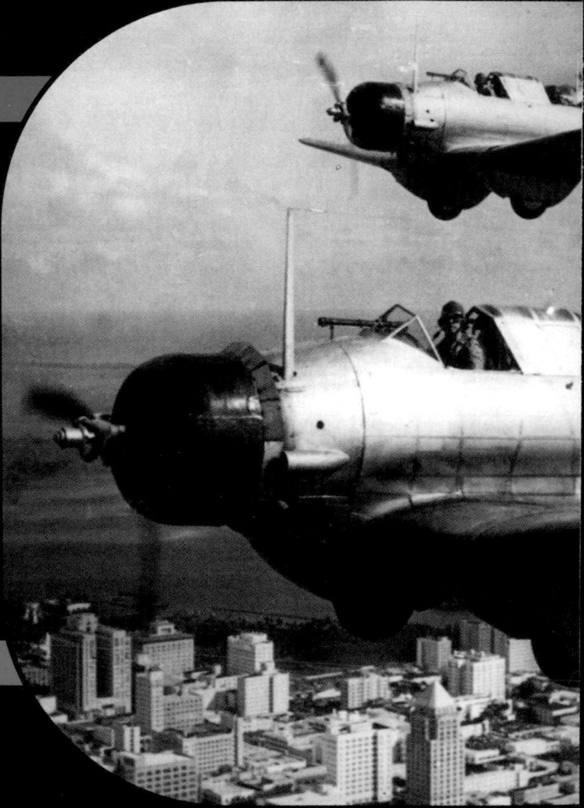

11

Fighter pilot is an attitude.
It is cockiness. It is aggressiveness.
It is self-confidence.
It is a streak of rebelliousness,
and it is competitiveness.

BUT THERE'S SOMETHING
ELSE—THERE'S A SPARK.
THERE'S A DESIRE TO BE GOOD.
TO DO WELL IN THE EYES OF YOUR PEERS,
AND IN YOUR OWN MIND.

Harrier XV 280

FLYING IS AN ACT OF
CONQUEST, OF DEFEATING THE
MOST BASIC AND POWERFUL
FORCES OF NATURE. IT UNITES
THE VIOLENT RAGE AND BRUTE
POWER OF JET ENGINES WITH
THE INFINITESIMAL
TOLERANCES OF THE COCKPIT.

15

Britannia airliner

BUTTONS...CHECK.
DIALS...CHECK.
SWITCHES...CHECK.
LEVERS...CHECK.
LITTLE COLORED LIGHTS...CHECK.

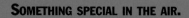
SOMETHING SPECIAL IN THE AIR.

PILOTS TAKE NO SPECIAL JOY IN WALKING. PILOTS LIKE FLYING.

Orbiter space shuttle on the back of a 747

AVIATION IS FOR GROWN MEN, ALERT, STRONG,

AND ABOVE ALL CAPABLE OF ENDURANCE.

"Scylla," an Imperial Airways airliner

27

I can't believe **ALL** the instructions are in Japanese.

FLYING IS THE PERFECT VOCATION FOR A
MAN WHO WANTS TO FEEL LIKE A BOY,
BUT NOT FOR ONE WHO STILL IS.

SPACE IN WHICH TO
MANEUVER IN THE AIR, UNLIKE
FIGHTING ON LAND OR SEA,
IS PRACTICALLY UNLIMITED,
AND...ANY NUMBER OF AIRPLANES
OPERATING DEFENSIVELY
WOULD SELDOM STOP
A DETERMINED ENEMY
FROM GETTING THROUGH.

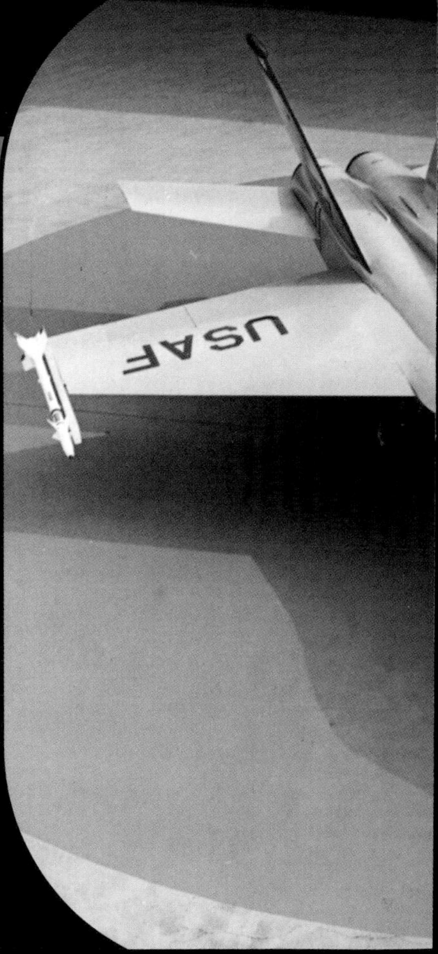

THEREFORE THE AIRPLANE WAS, AND IS, ESSENTIALLY AN INSTRUMENT OF ATTACK, NOT DEFENSE.

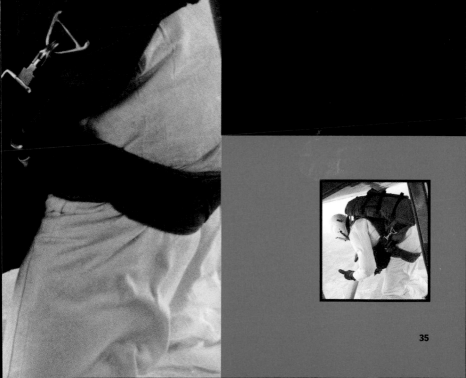

Bristol Brabazon I

I'VE NEVER KNOWN AN INDUSTRY THAT CAN GET INTO

OUR MODERN AIRPLANES FLY SO FAST WE DON'T HAVE TIME TO GET ACQUAINTED WITH ALL THE STEWARDESSES.

USAF B-36 bomber

213570

BUT THERE'S SOMETHING MORE MAJESTIC AND STABLE
ABOUT THE BIG BOMBERS WHICH A PILOT BEGINS TO LOVE.

THE OWNER'S GUIDE THAT COMES WITH A
$500 REFRIGERATOR MAKES MORE SENSE

**THAN ONE THAT COMES WITH
A $50 MILLION AIRLINER.**

JET NOISE:
THE SOUND
OF FREEDOM.

ONE PEEK IS WORTH A THOUSAND INSTRUMENT CROSS CHECKS.

Jets on a Vickers VC 10

**F-111 swing wing
tactical fighter plane**

AIRPLANE:
LOTS OF PARTS FLYING IN CLOSE FORMATION.

A FIGHTER PILOT IS A MAN IN LOVE WITH FLYING. A FIGHTER PILOT SEES NOT A CLOUD BUT BEAUTY. NOT THE GROUND BUT SOMETHING REMOTE FROM HIM, SOMETHING THAT HE DOESN'T BELONG TO AS LONG AS HE IS AIRBORNE. HE'S A MAN WHO WANTS TO BE SECOND BEST TO NO ONE.

A MODERN, AUTONOMOUS, AND THOROUGHLY TRAINED AIR FORCE IN BEING

AT ALL TIMES WILL NOT ALONE BE SUFFICIENT,
BUT WITHOUT IT THERE CAN BE NO NATIONAL SECURITY.

THINGS AND THINKING OF SO MANY OTHER THINGS, ALL AT THE SAME TIME.

PIT OF YOUR STOMACH.

LEARNING THE SECRET OF FLIGHT FROM A BIRD WAS A GOOD DEAL LIKE LEARNING THE SECRET OF MAGIC FROM A MAGICIAN. AFTER YOU ONCE KNOW THE TRICK AND KNOW WHAT TO LOOK FOR, YOU SEE THINGS THAT YOU DID NOT NOTICE WHEN YOU DID NOT KNOW EXACTLY WHAT TO LOOK FOR.

Concorde

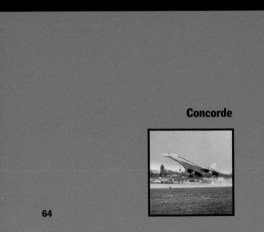

AN AIRPLANE WILL PROBABLY FLY A
LITTLE BIT OVERWEIGHT BUT IT SURE
WON'T FLY WITHOUT FUEL.

US C-5 Galaxy

Harrier V-STOL

THERE IS NO EXCUSE FOR AN AIRPLANE UNLESS IT WILL FLY FAST.

Giant Empire flying
boat "Capella"

73

AN AIRPLANE IS NO MORE THAN A FEW
NUTS AND BOLTS HELD TOGETHER ON A
WING AND A PRAYER.

Boeing 747

...IS SO BIG THAT IT
HAS BEEN SAID THAT
IT DOES NOT FLY;
THE EARTH MERELY DROPS
OUT FROM UNDER IT.

77

EAGLES MAY SOAR BUT A PIG NEVER GOT SUCKED INTO A JET ENGINE.

U.S. AIR FORCE
31529

F-100 Super Sabre

WE ARE ALL IN THE GUTTER
BUT SOME OF US ARE
LOOKING AT THE STARS.

Charles A. Lindbergh's "Spirit of St. Louis"

Firefighter

**TAKE POSSESSION OF THE AIR;
SUBMIT THE ELEMENTS;
PENETRATE THE LAST
REDOUBTS OF NATURE.**

87

AVIATION IN ITSELF IS INHERENTLY DANGEROUS. BUT TO AN EVEN GREATER DEGREE THAN THE SEA, IT IS TERRIBLY UNFORGIVING OF ANY CARELESSNESS, INCAPACITY, OR NEGLECT.

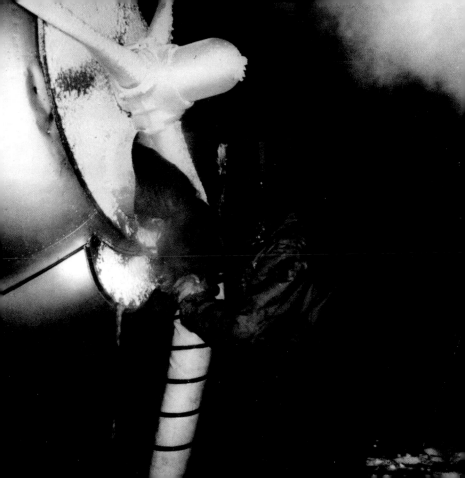

Hawker-Siddley Harrier Jump Jet

NO ONE HAS EVER COLLIDED WITH THE SKY.

Lockhead Blackbird

THAT WILBUR WRIGHT IS IN POSSESSION OF A POWER
WHICH CONTROLS THE FATE OF NATIONS IS BEYOND DISPUTE.

Skybolt missile

SHUT THE DOOR AND STRAP ME IN
ENCLOSED WITHIN A WORLD OF TIN
ENGINES RUMBLE, THEN REV HIGH
OH MY GOD WE'RE STARTING TO FLY.

The incomplete hull of a
Hughes Hercules 4

I LAUGH TO SEE YOUR TINY WORLD,
YOUR TOYS OF SHIPS, YOUR CARS.
I ROVE AN ENDLESS ROAD UNFURLED,
WHERE THE MILESTONES ARE THE STARS.

WHEN ONCE YOU HAVE TASTED FLIGHT,
YOU WILL FOREVER WALK THE EARTH
WITH YOUR EYES TURNED SKYWARD,
FOR THERE YOU HAVE BEEN,
AND THERE YOU WILL ALWAYS
LONG TO RETURN.

B-17 Flying Fortress

PICTURE CREDITS

All images Hulton Getty Picture Collection

Page 8/9: Replica of "Spirit of St. Louis," the aircraft in which Charles A. Lindbergh made the first solo and non-stop fight across the Atlantic in 1927, next to Concorde at Roisst Airport, Paris, 1977.

Page 10/11: American dive-bombers flying over Miami on a training mission, 1941.

Page 12/13: Member of the 2nd Fighter–Interceptor Squadron stands by his fighter plane at McGuire Air Force Base, New Jersey, circa 1950.

Page 14/15: Harrier XV 280 jet plane launching from the ski ramp at RAF Bedford, England, circa 1965.

Page 16/17: Giant jet housings of the American F-111 swing wing tactical fighter plane at the RAF station at Wethersfield, England, 1967.

Page 18/19: Flight deck of a Britannia airliner, 1955.

Page 20/21: Passenger aircraft flown by American Airlines, Inc., circa 1950.

Page 22/23: NASA's Orbiter space shuttle takes to the air on the back of a 747 airplane, 1977.

Page 24/25: Flight Lieutenant David Cyster ready to embark on his trip to Darwin, Australia in a 1941 Tiger Moth, 1978.

Page 26/27: The three propellers of "Scylla," an Imperial Airways airliner, on the tarmac at Croydon Airport, England, circa 1935.

Page 28/29: Bi-plane being serviced, 1934.

Page 30/31: Stunt man climbs a ladder from a moving car to an airplane from the film "The Great Waldo Pepper," 1974.

Page 32/33: Northrup YF-17, 1974.

Page 34/35: Member of the Delaware Valley Parachute Club prepares to jump, circa 1955.

Page 36/37: The Bristol Brabazon I at London Airport, 1950.

Page 38/39: Stewardesses on Southwest Airlines in Texas stand in front of planes belonging to the airline, circa 1980.

Page 40/41: USAF Lockhead ultrasonic jet fighter F-104A, 1956.

Page 42/43: USAF B-36 bomber, 1946.

Page 44/45: Ground crew replacing the oil tank filler cap after checking the oil level of the Avro Delta 707B, the British delta wing prototype jet aircraft, 1951.

Page 46/47: A General Electric TF 39 turbofan engine is subjected to hurricane force winds and severe icing conditions in a test center at Peebles in Ohio, 1968.

Page 48/49: Underside of two Rolls Royce Conway R CO 42 by-pass jets on a Vickers 10 passenger plane, 1964.

Page 50/51: Bristol Brabazon I in flight, 1950.

Page 52/53: A completed B-47 Stratojet airplane being rolled off the assembly line

ATTRIBUTIONS

Page 8/9: Eastern Airlines advertising slogan.

Page 12/13; Brigadier General Robin Olds, USAF.

Page 14/15: Thomas Petzinger.

Page 18/19: Anon.

Page 20/21: American Airlines advertising slogan.

Page 22/23: Neil Armstrong.

Page 24/25: Charles Turner.

Page 28/29: Anon.

Page 30/31: Air Vice-Marshal J. E. "Johnnie" Johnson, RAF.

Page 32/33: Anon.

Page 34/35: To bale out of an aircraft by parachute.

Page 36/37: Robert Six, founder of Continental Airlines.

Page 38/39: Anon.

Page 42/43: Sir Ross Smith, K. B. E.

Page 44/45: Anon.

Page 46/47: Anon.

Page 48/49: Anon.

Page 50/51: Anne Morrow Lindbergh.

Page 54/55: Anon.

Page 56/57: Brigadier General Robin Olds, USAF.

Page 60/61: General H. H. "Hap" Arnold, USAF.

Page 62/63: Dusty McTavish.

Page 64/65: Orville Wright.

Page 66/67: Anon.

Page 68/69: Roscoe Turner.

Page 70/71: Anon.

Page 74/75: Anon.

Page 76/77: Captain Ned Wilson.

Page 80/81: Anon.

Page 82/83: Oscar Wilde.

Page 84/85: Charles A. Lindbergh.

Page 86/87: Romain Rolland.

Page 88/89: Anon.

Page 90/91: Anon.

Page 94/95: Anon.

Page 96/97: Major B. F. S. Baden-Powell.

Page 100/101: Gill Hamper from " To Panic and Beyond."

Page 102/103: Marcel Dassault.

Page 104/105: Gordon Boshell from "The Aeroplane."

Page 106/107: Leonardo da Vinci.

Poem by Gill Hamper used with permission from Gill Hamper and Poetry Now 1996.